KETANJI BROWN JACKSON

KETANJI BROWN JACKSON

First Black Woman on the US Supreme Court

Heather E. Schwartz

LERNER PUBLICATIONS ◆ MINNEAPOLIS

Lerner Publications Company
An imprint of Lerner Publishing Group, Inc.
241 First Avenue North
Minneapolis, MN 55401 USA

For reading levels and more information, look up this title at www.lernerbooks.com.

Main body text set in Rotis Serif Std 55 Regular. Typeface provided by Adobe Systems.

Designer: Lauren Cooper
Lerner team: Sue Marquis

Library of Congress Cataloging-in-Publication Data

Names: Schwartz, Heather E., author.
Title: Ketanji Brown Jackson : first black woman on the US Supreme Court / Heather E. Schwartz.
Description: Minneapolis : Lerner Publications , 2023. | Series: Gateway biographies | Includes bibliographical references and index. | Audience: Ages 9–14 | Audience: Grades 4–6 | Summary: "Ketanji Brown Jackson is an American jurist and the first Black woman to serve on the US Supreme Court. Learn about her history of public service and how she rose to the highest court in the US"— Provided by publisher.
Identifiers: LCCN 2022024558 (print) | LCCN 2022024559 (ebook) | ISBN 9781728476599 (library binding) | ISBN 9781728486352 (paperback) | ISBN 9781728482828 (ebook)
Subjects: LCSH: Jackson, Ketanji Brown, 1970-–Juvenile literature. | Women judges–United States–Biography–Juvenile literature. | African American women judges–Biography–Juvenile literature. | United States. Supreme Court–Officials and employees–Juvenile literature.
Classification: LCC KF8745.J25 S39 2023 (print) | LCC KF8745.J25 (ebook) | DDC 347.73/2634 [B]–dc23/eng/20220801

LC record available at https://lccn.loc.gov/2022024558
LC ebook record available at https://lccn.loc.gov/2022024559

Manufactured in the United States of America
1-52240-50680-8/16/2022

TABLE OF CONTENTS

Judge Ketanji Brown Jackson

In March 2022 Ketanji Brown Jackson sat before a microphone, ready to answer questions from US senators. She knew they wanted to find out more about her. She'd been nominated for the US Supreme Court, the highest court in the nation, and they wanted to be sure she was the right person for the job.

Jackson had spent much of her career as a judge. She might have expected questions about previous cases she'd ruled on and how she approached applying the law. But Republican senator Ted Cruz sat with a stack of children's books next to him. He flipped through the pages of a book called *Antiracist Baby* by Ibram X. Kendi. Cruz quoted aloud from several pages. Cruz said that the book was being taught at a private school in Washington, DC, where Jackson was a board member and where one of her

Jackson answers a question during her confirmation hearing in Washington, DC, on March 21, 2022.

daughters was a student. Cruz said the book's premise stated that babies are racist, and he asked Jackson if she agreed with that premise

Cruz was trying to prove that Jackson supported teaching critical race theory—that racism is a part of US history. Many Republicans had spoken out against it. If Cruz could get Jackson to say she supported it, then he and other Republicans could declare she was not qualified for the Supreme Court.

Jackson sighed and paused for a moment. The question had little to do with her work as a lawyer and a judge or what she might bring to the Supreme Court. It didn't have a connection to her position as a school board member either. She had no control over the school's curriculum. But she knew she had to answer honestly and keep her cool. She leaned toward the microphone.

"I do not believe that any child should be made to feel as though they are racist, or though they are not valued, or though they are less than, that they are victims, that they are oppressors," she said calmly. "I don't believe in any of that."

Senator Ted Cruz of Texas brought pages of *Antiracist Baby* to display while questioning Jackson.

The Major Parties

The US has two major political parties: the Democratic and Republican Parties. Democrats are usually more liberal and believe the government should do more for citizens. Republicans are usually more conservative and believe the government should step back and let individuals take more responsibility for themselves.

But Cruz wasn't satisfied. He held up another children's book about racism. He read passages to Jackson and then asked her whether she agreed. This time, Jackson didn't hesitate.

"Senator," she said. "I have not reviewed any of those books, any of those ideas. They don't come up in my work as a judge, which I am respectfully here to address."

Jackson smiled as she spoke, but her words were serious. Clearly, she could lead under pressure, advocate for herself, and respect others. These qualities made her a standout candidate for the Supreme Court.

Standout Student

Jackson was born Ketanji Onyika Brown on September 14, 1970, in Washington, DC. Her parents, Johnny and

The US Capitol Building (*center*) in Washington, DC

Ellery Brown, picked her name from a list sent to them by her aunt, a Peace Corps volunteer in West Africa. Ketanji Onyika means "lovely one" and honors the family's African heritage.

Ketanji's parents were both teachers. But when Ketanji was three, the family moved so her father could go to law school in Miami, Florida. As a preschooler, she sat next to him at the dining room table with a stack of coloring books to match his stack of law books. It was the beginning of her interest in studying the law.

Growing up in Florida, Ketanji enjoyed working hard to do her best, whether she was studying or pursuing her hobbies. She played piano for several years and loved reading and writing. She enjoyed public speaking from an early age. In first grade, she won a contest at a youth fair for reciting "For My People," a poem about Black courage by Margaret Walker.

Ketanji's mother became the principal of a public magnet high school, a school with a specialized curriculum. Her father became the chief attorney for the Miami-Dade school board. Both were successful and had grown up battling racism. They wanted their daughter to believe she could do anything and be anything she wanted to be.

Jackson's brother (*left*) and parents watch her confirmation hearing.

Little Brother

Ketanji was ten years old when her brother, Ketajh, was born. Growing up with so many years between them, Ketanji sometimes felt as though she was still an only child. As an adult, Ketajh Brown was a police officer before joining the Maryland National Guard. He eventually became a lawyer like Ketanji.

As Ketanji got older, she stood out as a star student who wasn't afraid to speak up for what she believed in. At Miami Palmetto High School, she was elected class president three years in a row. When US interior secretary Donald Hodel visited, Ketanji was one of a group of students who confronted him about oil drilling that damaged Florida's reefs. Ketanji was also one of the top students on the debate team, traveling the country to compete. One competition took her to Cambridge, Massachusetts, where she saw the Harvard University campus. She knew right away that she wanted to apply.

Back home, her guidance counselor wasn't encouraging and told her not to aim so high. But Ketanji didn't listen and applied to her dream school anyway. When she was accepted, her classmates celebrated with her.

"Every student was so happy for Ketanji and so proud of her accomplishment," recalled Ketanji's former classmate Richard B. Rosenthal. "Nobody was jealous, nobody was resentful . . . and nobody was at all surprised. Because she was Ketanji."

As high school ended, Ketanji faced a difficult choice. She could either attend her graduation ceremony or compete in a national debate tournament. Both were scheduled for the same day. But she felt she had to honor her commitment to her debate team, and that helped her to decide. She went to the tournament, where she won the competition and became a national champion. It was a fitting end to her high school career and an early step toward the goal she had written in her yearbook: "I want to go into law and eventually have a judicial appointment."

Harvard and Her Gap Year

In 1988 Jackson left her hometown for Harvard University. Her college years were a time for studying and expanding her horizons. She joined the Black Students Association and organized a study group focused on Black women writers. She also explored an interest in theater, performing in the show *Little Shop of Horrors*, writing the script for a play she starred in about the singer Billie Holiday, and earning a spot in an improv troupe called On Thin Ice. In one memorable drama class, she partnered for scene work with fellow student Matt Damon before he became a famous actor.

Harvard University in Cambridge, Massachusetts

Jackson went to Harvard to study government. But before long she was distracted by a situation that demanded her attention. When another student hung a Confederate flag out a dorm window, Black students felt attacked. The flag was a symbol of Black oppression, and they believed it was a message telling them they didn't belong on campus.

The Black Students Association jumped into action. They organized protests and passed out flyers and petitions. Jackson got involved with the protests. But she soon became known for finding a middle ground on issues and encouraging more moderate actions that brought people together. She also saw a bigger picture for Black students and their activism.

"While we were busy doing all of those very noble things, we were not in the library studying. I remember thinking how unfair it was to us," she said. "It was exactly what the student who had hung the flag really wanted: For us to be so distracted that we failed our classes and thereby reinforced the stereotype that we couldn't cut it at a place like Harvard."

Jackson worked hard to balance her activism with her personal goals at Harvard. And she encouraged her friends to do the same and make sure they kept up their studies. She taught them strategies for getting better grades, such as getting up early and using notecards to organize essays. Her methods worked, and one friend, Antoinette Coakley, was so impressed she predicted great success for Jackson—as the first Black woman Supreme Court justice.

"I thought if there was ever an opportunity for somcone that came from our background to ascend to those heights, it would be her. It had to be her. She had the keen intelligence, the brilliance, the ability to bring people together," Coakley said.

Aiming for a career in law, Jackson finished her undergraduate studies by writing a senior thesis. "The Hand of Oppression: Plea Bargaining Processes and the Coercion of Criminal Defendants" was focused on her ideas about fundamental flaws in the justice system. In 1992 she graduated magna cum laude, an academic honor earned by high-achieving students.

Before going to law school, Jackson worked as a reporter and researcher for *Time* magazine, where she wrote articles about economic policy and rising prescription drug prices. She also interned at the Neighborhood Defender Service of Harlem, a public defense practice that provided legal representation to people in need.

Law School and Beyond

In 1993 Jackson went to Harvard Law School. Once again, she was a top student and became an editor of the *Harvard Law Review*. In 1996 she graduated cum laude, a distinction of honor. That year she married her longtime boyfriend Patrick Graves Jackson. When she left school, she was ready to launch—both professionally and personally.

After graduation, Jackson clerked for two federal judges: US District Court judge for the District of Massachusetts Patti B. Saris and US Court of Appeals judge for the First Circuit Bruce M. Selya. Next, she went into private practice. Though she was interested in criminal law, she was a newlywed with rent, bills, and law school loans to pay. She had to be practical, and a job at a private company would pay more than a job in government. She went into

Meeting Her Match

While Jackson was an undergraduate student, she met a fellow classmate and started dating him. Patrick Graves Jackson was a white man whose family had gone to Harvard for seven generations. He had a very different background from Jackson's. Her parents had attended segregated schools as children. She was only the second generation in her family to go to college.

Her friends and parents got to know her boyfriend. They asked questions to make sure his goals and values matched hers.

Jackson and her husband at her confirmation hearing

private practice for a while before eventually clerking for Supreme Court justice Stephen Breyer. While all of her clerkships were interesting and valuable experiences, working within the Supreme Court had an incredible impact on her.

Jackson was eager to continue building her career in Washington, DC, but she also wanted to support her husband in his career. As a medical student, he was assigned to a residency in Boston, Massachusetts, so she went with him. It was the beginning of a lifelong journey to find balance between career and family. At the time of the move, she was three months pregnant. She found a job with a large law firm in Boston, and a few months later, her daughter Talia was born. Then the real juggling began.

Stephen Breyer in 1993, before he became a Supreme Court justice

Jackson's family, including her husband and two daughters, Leila (*center*) and Talia (*right, masked*)

"I don't think it is possible to overstate the degree of difficulty that many young women, and especially new mothers, face in the law firm context," Jackson said. "The hours are long. The workflow is unpredictable. You have little control over your time and your schedule."

Over the years, her family's needs kept changing. They moved from Boston to Washington, DC, and had another daughter, Leila, in 2005. Meanwhile, Jackson gained experience in legal work and took on more senior roles. Greater seniority meant she had more control over her time and was able to take jobs with more manageable projects. She was always working to prove herself and to find the personal and professional balance she needed.

"It was important to me to be seen as a person who worked hard and was good to work with," Jackson said. "As a young Black woman with a funny name, I already stood out, and so I invested heavily in doing what was required to build my brand within each organization I worked in."

Defending the Disadvantaged

In 2005 Jackson became an assistant federal public defender in Washington, DC. Her job focused on representing disadvantaged people in the justice system. Everyone in the US is entitled to a lawyer when accused of a crime, even if they can't pay or are clearly guilty. As a public defender, Jackson represented poor parents, teen victims of human trafficking, and people suspected of terrorism. She felt her work was a service that gave people their constitutional right to representation.

In 2007 Jackson returned to private practice, and two years later, then president Barack Obama nominated her to be a member of the US Sentencing Commission, an agency that develops sentencing policies for federal courts. If confirmed, she would help to set prison terms and work on other policies related to sentencing convicted criminals. Jackson's jobs all had been demanding. But as

We the People of the United States, in Order to form a more perfect Union, establish Justice, insure domestic Tranquility, provide for the common defence, promote the general Welfare, and secure the Blessings of Liberty to ourselves and our Posterity, do ordain and establish this Constitution for the United States of America.

Article. I

The US Constitution

she went through the confirmation process, her stress level ramped up considerably. She soon discovered a new way to calm her nerves.

"I actually taught myself to knit as a way to channel my nervous energy during that time," she said. "If anybody wants a scarf, I'm your source."

When the Senate confirmed her and Obama appointed her vice chair of the commission in February 2010, Jackson was relieved, happy, and grateful to get to work. Shaping federal sentencing policy was another way to help disadvantaged people. Laws surrounding drug crimes discriminated against poor Black people, and under Jackson's leadership, the commission reduced penalties for drug-related crimes. Those already in prison benefited from the change too. Many groups applauded the commission, including the National Association for the Advancement of Colored People (NAACP). To Jackson, it was a way to correct a historic injustice and make things right.

Jackson was doing what she had always wanted, making policies that set the law of the land and affected individual lives. But she wasn't nearly finished chasing her dreams. She had much more to contribute to her country.

Serving on the US District Court

In 2012 Obama nominated Jackson to join the US District Court for the District of Columbia. If confirmed, she would become a judge in federal civil and criminal trials. Republican senator Paul Ryan introduced her to the Senate. It was an unusual situation because she was a Democrat, but they happen to be related by marriage. Patrick Graves Jackson's twin brother and Ryan's wife's sister are married.

The NAACP

The National Association for the Advancement of Colored People was formed in 1909 to fight for equal rights, eliminate racism, and work for Black people's rights in voting, legal justice, education, and employment. It continues to work to protect all marginalized people's civil and human rights. More than two million activists are part of the organization.

A person in an NAACP shirt wore a pin with Jackson's likeness to celebrate her Supreme Court confirmation in April 2022.

Despite their differences, Ryan spoke highly of Jackson. "Our politics may differ, but my praise for Ketanji's intellect, for her character, for her integrity, it is unequivocal," he said. "She is an amazing person."

While she was honored to be nominated, Jackson knew her confirmation depended on Obama's victory in the upcoming presidential election. Waiting for months was a tense situation that ramped up on election night. Instead of knitting, this time, she sought refuge in a place where she wouldn't be able to see the news. Jackson relaxed at a spa, and when the votes were counted, Obama won reelection to a second term. Her path to the US District Court was clear. But more challenges lay ahead.

At her confirmation hearing, Republican senators grilled Jackson. Some people were surprised when her answers reflected previous court rulings instead of personal opinions. But many knew this was what they could expect from Jackson. She'd built a solid reputation based on her respect for the law. She was confirmed in March 2013.

Supporting Obama

Jackson, a Democrat, supported presidential candidate Barack Obama in 2008. She was an election poll monitor on behalf of the Obama for America presidential campaign during the primary and general elections. She identified personally with Democratic politics, but in her work as a lawyer and a judge she knew she had to be impartial.

The E. Barrett Prettyman United States Courthouse in Washington, DC, houses the US District Court where Jackson served.

Jackson judged several notable cases while serving on the US District Court. In 2015 she ruled in favor of a Deaf inmate who was denied hearing aids and sign-language interpreters while he was in prison. Basing her decision on the Americans with Disabilities Act, she made it clear that the law was there to protect all disabled people, including prisoners.

"Incarceration inherently involves the relinquishment of many privileges; however, prisoners still retain certain civil rights, including protections against disability discrimination," she wrote.

Another high-profile case occurred in 2017. A man entered a Washington, DC, pizza restaurant and fired a gun, claiming he was there to rescue imprisoned children. But no children were being held against their will at the restaurant. And the man had broken the law, putting people in danger. The case made national news. The man was convicted, and Jackson was the judge to decide his sentence.

Strong Supporter

In 2016 Supreme Court justice Antonin Scalia died, leaving a vacancy on the Supreme Court. Jackson's then eleven-year-old daughter Leila wrote a letter to President Obama, recommending her mother for the job. "She is determined, honest, and never breaks a promise to anyone, even if there are other things she'd rather do," she wrote. "She can demonstrate commitment, and is loyal and never brags."

Jackson's daughter Leila sits behind her at her confirmation hearing on March 22, 2022.

Though the man's lawyer argued for eighteen months in prison, Jackson took a stronger stance and gave him four years. She said that part of her decision came from how his actions might inspire others to act violently. The sentence also sent a message about how the law works in the US.

"No matter how well-intentioned, people are not allowed to take matters into their own hands," she said.

Leading with the Law

In 2016 Donald Trump was elected president of the United States. Jackson continued serving on the US District Court, and her job hadn't changed. She still had to make fair and impartial rulings based on the law. But now, she would be called upon to do so in cases involving the country's highest leader because questions about Trump's actions were being called into court.

A case in 2018 involved executive orders Trump had signed to limit the power of labor unions. Under his orders, it was easier for managers to fire federal employees and more difficult for workers to fight back. The labor unions sued to block the orders. When the case landed in Jackson's court, she ruled in favor of the labor unions. Her ruling went against the president, but she based it on the law. In her decision she wrote that Trump's executive orders undermined the Federal Service Labor-Management Relations Statute, a law that protects workers.

Jackson in 2019

In 2019 Jackson found herself ruling in more cases focused on presidential power. When the Trump administration planned to expand fast-track deportations of undocumented immigrants, she blocked the new policy. She questioned the president's authority to make new policies too quickly, which she said went against the Administrative Procedure Act. She also pointed out that this plan would affect real people's lives.

"There is no question in this Court's mind that an agency cannot possibly conduct reasoned, non-arbitrary decision making concerning policies that might impact real people and not take such real life circumstances into account," she wrote.

That year she ruled in another case involving a former Trump adviser. The adviser had been ordered to testify before Congress about possible Russian interference in the 2016 presidential election. Trump didn't want his adviser to testify and claimed he didn't have to under the law. Once again, Jackson saw things differently.

"Presidents are not kings," she wrote. "This means that they do not have subjects, bound by loyalty or blood, whose destiny they are entitled to control. Rather, in this land of liberty, it is indisputable that current and former employees of the White House work for the People of the United States, and that they take an oath to protect and defend the Constitution of the United States."

Jackson's rulings didn't always stick. An appeals court overturned her 2018 decision in favor of labor unions as well as her 2019 decision that would have protected undocumented immigrants. But that didn't mean her rulings were wrong. Different courts and judges are allowed to interpret the law in different ways.

Through her rulings on the US District Court, people were getting a good idea of how Jackson interpreted the law and how she might decide future cases. Everything she did was on record. She was changing the course of history, establishing herself as a leader, and leaning into a career that was taking her to increasingly powerful positions.

Changes in the Nation

In 2020, when Joe Biden won the presidential election, Trump refused to accept defeat. He and other Republicans insisted the vote was rigged. On January 6, 2021, a mob of Trump supporters stormed the US Capitol to disrupt the certification of votes and keep Biden out of office. Their actions shocked the nation and would lead to lengthy investigations about who was to blame.

Jackson soon learned she would play a part in those investigations. In February, Biden nominated her to join the US Court of Appeals. The court is above the US District Court and just below the US Supreme Court. Jackson was then appointed to a three-judge panel to investigate Trump's role in the events of January 6.

Meanwhile, Jackson's career continued to rise. In March she was awarded the Constance Baker Motley Award, named for one of her heroes. The former New York State senator was the first Black woman to serve as a federal judge. The award honors a woman attorney of color with a strong record of giving back to the community. Jackson was excited that she could inspire other young women the way Motley had inspired her. When the award was presented, she offered advice to an audience of law students and others at the start of their law careers.

Jackson at a Senate Judiciary Committee confirmation hearing on April 28, 2021

"The key to success in this business, or any other business for that matter, is believing in yourself and your own ability to do good work, no matter what others might think or say," she said.

In January 2022, another major event shook up national politics. Supreme Court justice Stephen Breyer decided to retire after twenty-seven years on the court. He was the oldest member and could have stayed. But stepping down meant Biden would have the chance to pick a replacement. Biden quickly said that he planned to nominate a Black woman, the first Black woman ever nominated for the position.

The media made guesses about whom Biden might pick. Jackson's name came up among other highly qualified candidates. Some thought Vice President Kamala Harris might be Biden's top choice. By February the president had interviewed Jackson for the position. His list narrowed down to three: Jackson, California Supreme Court justice Leondra Kruger, and South Carolina District Court judge J. Michelle Childs. As promised, they were all Black, women judges with solid records.

Biden had until the end of February to make his final decision and choose a nominee for a lifetime appointment on the country's highest court.

Inspiring Women

Jackson has been lifted up by many supportive and inspiring women along the way, including family members, teachers, coaches, and judges. She also lists women she's never met among her heroes. They include Sojourner Truth, Harriet Tubman, Indira Gandhi, Susan B. Anthony, Amelia Earhart, Marie Curie, Shirley Chisholm, Belva Lockwood, Constance Baker Motley, and Eleanor Roosevelt.

Joining the Supreme Court

On February 25, 2022, Biden nominated Jackson to the Supreme Court. If confirmed, she would become the first Black woman and the first former public defender to serve on the court. She would be ruling on controversial cases from lower courts and making final decisions. Her work would create lasting laws that would affect generations of Americans.

"For too long, our government and our courts haven't looked like America," Biden said. "And I believe it's time that we have a court that reflects the full talents and greatness of our nation with a nominee of extraordinary qualifications."

Jackson's longtime Harvard friends were ecstatic. They cried and shouted, but they weren't surprised. Their predictions for her had come true. And after all of her work in the years leading up to this day, Jackson was humbled and grateful.

"If I am fortunate enough to be confirmed as the next associate justice of the Supreme Court of the United States, I can only hope that my life and career, my love of this country and the Constitution, and my commitment to upholding the rule of law and the sacred principles upon which this great nation was founded will inspire future generations of Americans," she said.

Her confirmation seemed likely. But first, Jackson had to face a gauntlet of confirmation hearings. Members of the US Senate would be allowed to question her about her previous legal decisions, her personal values, and anything else they believed might influence her rulings and opinions as a Supreme Court justice. Previous confirmation hearings for judges, especially in the years leading up to Jackson's, had been contentious.

The hearings began on March 22, and Jackson made an opening statement. Her husband and daughters were there to support her. She vowed to decide Supreme Court cases based on facts and to defend the Constitution. She told the senators she would not allow her personal values to influence her decisions.

Jackson withstood hours of questioning and secured a majority vote to be confirmed as a Supreme Court justice.

The senators had the opportunity to speak too. Democratic senators supported her. They focused on how Jackson could add to the court with her background in public defense and her perspective as someone belonging to an underrepresented group. Republican senators took a different approach. They talked about how a recent conservative Supreme Court nominee, Justice Brett Kavanaugh, was treated during his hearings. They said his treatment was unfair and disgraceful. They promised to be more respectful of Jackson over the next few days.

On the second and third days of the hearings, Jackson was questioned for hours. She was asked about important issues that mattered to both Democrats and Republicans, including her stance on racism, her sentencing record on criminal cases, and her philosophy as a judge. During many tense moments, Republican senators tried to prove she wasn't fit for the court and continued questioning her after their time was up.

On the last day of the hearings, March 24, there were no more questions for Jackson. Instead, representatives of the American Bar Association spoke about her. The association focuses on education, just laws, diversity, and the elimination of bias in the legal profession. The representatives spoke glowingly of Jackson's career. Only the vote was left.

On April 7, every Democratic senator voted in favor of confirming Jackson, while only three Republicans did. Vice President Kamala Harris announced the final count of 53 to 47, and Jackson was confirmed. The Democratic

Jackson and Vice President Kamala Harris celebrate Jackson's confirmation in April 2022.

senators broke into an extended round of applause and cheers. Jackson's journey and her confirmation were cause for celebration.

Jackson's remarks after the vote were filled with gratitude for her family and others who supported her. She also recognized that her personal victory was part of a historic moment, and a victory for the nation too.

"I have dedicated my career to public service because I love this country and our Constitution and the rights that make us free," Jackson said. "It has taken 232 years and 115 prior appointments for a Black woman to be selected to serve on the Supreme Court of the United States. But we've made it. We've made it. All of us."

Jackson's confirmation meant she would become a Supreme Court justice once Stephen Breyer left his position. On June 30, 2022, Breyer officially retired,

Supporters gave out items including these glasses reading "Justice Jackson" to celebrate Jackson's confirmation in April 2022.

Jackson took the Constitutional Oath on June 30, 2022, to officially become the first Black woman on the US Supreme Court.

and Jackson was sworn in. In a ceremony led by Chief Justice John Roberts, Jackson took an oath to uphold the Constitution in her work. She rose to finally take her place on the US Supreme Court.

IMPORTANT DATES

1970	Ketanji Brown Jackson is born.
1992	She graduates from Harvard University.
1996	She graduates from Harvard Law School and marries Patrick Graves Jackson.
2001	She moves with her family to Boston.
	Her daughter Talia is born.
2005	Jackson becomes an assistant federal public defender in Washington, DC.
2010	She is confirmed to the US Sentencing Commission and appointed vice chair.
2013	Jackson joins the US District Court for the District of Columbia.
2016	Donald Trump is elected president of the United States.

2020	Joe Biden is elected president of the United States.
2021	Jackson joins the US Court of Appeals.
2022	Supreme Court justice Stephen Breyer announces his retirement.
	Biden nominates Jackson to the US Supreme Court.
	Jackson is confirmed.
	Jackson takes her position on the US Supreme Court.

SOURCE NOTES

9 "WATCH: Sen. Ted Cruz Presses Ketanji [Brown Jackson] on Critical Race Theory," YouTube video, 4:32, posted by PBS NewsHour, March 22, 2022, https://www.youtube.com/watch?v=TkUs6B9DE_k.

10 "WATCH: Sen. Ted Cruz."

13–14 Liane Morejon and Andrea Torres, "Miami Palmetto Students Feel Proud to Be Associated with Ketanji Brown Jackson," Local10.com, last modified April 8, 2022, https://www.local10.com/news/local/2022/04/07/miami-palmetto-students-feel-proud-to-be-associated-with-ketanji-brown-jackson/#:~:text=Miami%20Palmetto%20Senior%20High%20School%20students%20said%20they%20were%20inspired,she%20was%20going%20to%20Harvard.

14 Morejon and Torres.

16 Laura Doan, "Judge Ketanji Brown Jackson's Friends from Harvard Not Surprised by Her Supreme Court Nomination: 'It Had to Be Her,'" CBS News, March 18, 2022, https://www.cbsnews.com/news/supreme-court-ketanji-brown-jackson-friends-harvard/.

16 Marc Fisher, Ann E. Marimow, and Lori Rozsa, "How Ketanji Brown Jackson Found a Path between Confrontation and Compromise," *Washington Post*, February 25, 2022, https://www.washingtonpost.com/politics/2022/02/25/ketanji-brown-jackson-miami-family-parents/.

20 "35th Edith House Lecture: Ketanji Brown Jackson, U.S. District Court for the District of Columbia," YouTube video, 34:32, posted by University of Georgia Law School, March 2, 2017, https://www.youtube.com/watch?v=jXFerWhSckA&t=771s&ab_channel=UniversityofGeorgiaSchoolofLaw.

21 Fisher, Marimow, and Rozsa, "How Ketanji Brown Jackson Found a Path."

22 "Edith House Lecture," YouTube video.

24 Fisher, Marimow, and Rozsa, "How Ketanji Brown Jackson Found a Path."

26 Ketanji Brown Jackson, Pierce v. Dist. of Columbia, CaseText, September 11, 2015, https://casetext.com/case/pierce-v-dist-of-columbia.

27 Eric Fayeulle, "Judge Ketanji Brown Jackson's Daughter Once Asked Obama to Put Her Mom on the High Court, ABC News, March 3, 2022, https://abcnews.go.com/Politics/judge-ketanji-brown-jacksons-daughter-asked-obama-put/story?id=83235587.

28 Geneva Sands, "'Pizzagate' Shooter Sentenced to 4 Years in Prison, Judge Describes 'Breathtaking' Recklessness," ABC News, June 22, 2017, https://abcnews.go.com/US/pizzagate-shooter-sentenced-years-prison-judge-describes-breathtaking/story?id=48213928.

30 "Notable Opinions by High Court Nominee Ketanji Brown Jackson," AP News, March 20, 2022, https://apnews.com/article/immigration-biden-us-supreme-court-business-donald-trump-e2ae42333212f33fbbf9eaf756100d48.

30 "Notable Opinions."

32 "Judge Ketanji Brown Jackson and Erika E. Vera Livas '16 Honored at Constance Baker Motley Gala," Columbia Law School, April 13, 2021, https://www.law.columbia.edu/news/archive/judge-ketanji-brown-jackson-and-erika-e-vera-livas-16-honored-2021-constance-baker-motley-gala.

34 Jeff Mason, Jarrett Renshaw, and Lawrence Hurley, "Biden Picks Ketanji Brown Jackson as Historic U.S. Supreme Court Nominee," Reuters, February 26, 2022, https://www.reuters.com/world/us/biden-announce-us-supreme-court-pick-friday-white-house-sources-2022-02-25/.

34 "Judge Ketanji Brown Jackson Remarks on Historic Supreme Court Confirmation," YouTube video, 19:13, posted by ABC News, April 8, 2022, https://www.youtube.com/watch?v=6eOWKuYzb98.

38 "Judge Ketanji Brown Jackson Remarks."

SELECTED BIBLIOGRAPHY

Carlisle, Madeleine. "What Ketanji Brown Jackson Could Bring to the Supreme Court." *Time*, February 25, 2022. https://time.com/6151590/ketanji-brown-jackson-supreme-court-profile/.

Duignan, Brian. "United States Capitol Attack of 2021." *Encyclopaedia Britannica Online*. Accessed June 24, 2022. https://www.britannica.com/event/United-States-Capitol-attack-of-2021.

Fayeulle, Eric. "Judge Ketanji Brown Jackson's Daughter Once Asked Obama to Put Her Mom on the High Court. ABC News, March 3, 2022. https://abcnews.go.com/Politics/judge-ketanji-brown-jacksons-daughter-asked-obama-put/story?id=83235587.

"Judge Ketanji Brown Jackson Remarks on Historic Supreme Court Confirmation." YouTube video, 19:13. Posted by ABC News, April 8, 2022. https://www.youtube.com/watch?v=6eOWKuYzb98.

"Judge Ketanji Brown Jackson's Friends from Harvard Not Surprised by Her Supreme Court Nomination: 'It Had to Be Her.'" CBS News, March 18, 2022. https://www.cbsnews.com/news/supreme-court-ketanji-brown-jackson-friends-harvard/.

Kendi, Ibram X. *Antiracist Baby*. New York: Kokila, 2020.

"Notable Opinions by High Court Nominee Ketanji Brown Jackson." AP News, March 20, 2022. https://apnews.com/article/immigration-biden-us-supreme-court-business-donald-trump-e2ae42333212f33fbbf9eaf756100d48.

"The Senate Confirms Ketanji Brown Jackson to Serve on the Supreme Court." White House. Accessed June 24, 2022. https://www.whitehouse.gov/kbj/.

"35th Edith House Lecture: Ketanji Brown Jackson, US District Court for the District of Columbia." YouTube video, 34:37. Posted by University of Georgia School of Law, March 23, 2017. https://www.youtube.com/watch?v=jXFerWhSckA&t=771s.

"WATCH: Sen. Ted Cruz Presses Ketanji [Brown Jackson] on Critical Race Theory." YouTube video, 4:32. Posted by *PBS NewsHour*, March 22, 2022. https://www.youtube.com/watch?v=TkUs6B9DE_k.

Williams, Pete. "Justice Stephen Breyer to Retire from Supreme Court, Paving Way for Biden Appointment." NBC News, January 26, 2022. https://www.nbcnews.com/politics/supreme-court/justice-stephen-breyer-retire-supreme-court-paving-way-biden-appointment-n1288042.

LEARN MORE

Britannica Kids: United States Government
https://kids.britannica.com/kids/article/United-States-Government/353887

Harvard University
https://www.harvard.edu

Schwartz, Heather E. *Joe Biden: From Scranton to the White House.* Minneapolis: Lerner Publications, 2021.

Sherman, Jill. *Donald Trump: Outspoken Personality and President.* Minneapolis: Lerner Publications, 2017.

Supreme Court of the United States
https://www.supremecourt.gov/about/about.aspx

Weber, M. *Political Parties.* Mankato, MN: Child's World, 2021

INDEX

PHOTO ACKNOWLEDGMENTS

Image credits: Kent Nishimura/Los Angeles Times/Getty Images, pp. 2, 12, 18; American Photo Archive/Alamy Stock Photo, p. 6; Michael McCoy/Bloomberg/Getty Images, p. 8; Win McNamee/Getty Images, pp. 9, 27; Glowimages/Getty Images, p. 11; Roman Babakin/Getty Images, p. 15; Ira Wyman/Sygma/Getty Images, p. 19; Tom Williams/CQ-Roll Call, Inc/Getty Images, p. 20; National Archives at Washington, DC, p. 22; Anna Moneymaker/Getty Images, pp. 24, 37, 38; Maurice Savage/Alamy Stock Photo, p. 26; Bill O'Leary/The Washington Post/Getty Images, p. 29; Kevin Lamarque/Reuters/Bloomberg/Getty Images, p. 32; Julia Nikhinson/Bloomberg/Getty Images, p. 35; Fred Schilling/Collection of the Supreme Court of the United States/Getty Images, p. 39.

Design element: janniwet/shutterstock.com.

Cover image: Kevin Lamarque/Pool/ABACAPRESS.COM/Alamy Stock Photo.